FOOTBALL SUPERSTARS

VAN DIJK RULES

WELBECK

Published in 2020 by Welbeck Children's Books
An imprint of Hachette Children's Group
Part of Hodder & Stoughton Limited
Carmelite House, 50 Victoria Embankment
London EC4Y 0DZ
An Hachette UK Company
www.hachette.co.uk
www.hachettechildrens.co.uk

ISBN: 978-1-78312-565-4

Writer: Simon Mugford
Designer and Illustrator: Dan Green
Design Manager: Sam James
Senior Commissioning Editor: Suhel Ahmed
Production: Arlene Alexander

A catalogue record for this book is available from the British Library.

MIX
Paper | Supporting responsible forestry
FSC® C104740

Printed in the UK
10 9 8 7 6 5

Statistics and records correct as of June 2020

FOOTBALL SUPERSTARS

VAN DIJK RULES

SIMON MUGFORD DAN GREEN

CONTENTS

CHAPTER 1

HEY, VIRGIL!

VAN DIJK! VAN DIJK!

Virgil van Dijk is an

AWESOME FOOTBALLER

He is the ***ROCK*** at the centre of the Liverpool defence. Virgil has won the **CHAMPIONS LEAGUE** and **PREMIER LEAGUE** and is captain of the **Dutch** national team.

VAN DIJK is a GIANT in world football.
This book is all about him!

SO, WHAT MAKES VAN DIJK SO VERY GOOD?

Vision
He almost always knows what his opponent is going to do.

Height and strength
Towers above his opponents to win possession.

Passing
Gets the ball to his team-mates with his pinpoint passing.

Set-pieces
The master of scoring goals from free-kicks and corners.

Leadership
Cool and calm under pressure, he leads from the back.

VAN DIJK
IS PROBABLY THE BEST
DEFENDER IN THE WORLD!

VAN DIJK IN NUMBERS

So, **how good** is **Virgil van Dijk?**

Let's look at some **numbers:**

1 . . . PREMIER LEAGUE win

1 . . . CHAMPIONS LEAGUE win

2 . . . SCOTTISH PREMIERSHIP wins

1 . . . Players' Player of the Year Award

1

. . . Premier League Player of the Season Award

More than **100 APPEARANCES** for **Liverpool** and **Celtic**

Estimated **£75 MILLION** transfer to Liverpool

Over 9 MILLION followers on Instagram!

VAN DIJK I.D

NAME: *Virgil van Dijk*

NICKNAME: *VVD, The Dyke*

DATE OF BIRTH: *8 July 1991*

PLACE OF BIRTH: *Breda, Netherlands*

HEIGHT: *1.93 m*

POSITION: *Centre-back*

CLUBS: *Groningen, Celtic, Southampton, Liverpool*

NATIONAL TEAM: *Netherlands*

LEFT OR RIGHT-FOOTED: *Right*

CHAPTER 2

BREDA BOY

Virgil van Dijk was born on **8 July 1991.**

He grew up in the city of **Breda,** in the south of the **Netherlands.**

Breda church, **Grote Kerk**
Breda is famous for its history and beautiful old buildings.
Nice threads!

Virgil's mum, Hellen, was born in **Suriname,** a small country in **South America.**

Some **VERY** famous Dutch footballers have their family roots in Suriname:

Former Ajax and Barcelona striker, **Patrick Kluivert**

Ex-Juventus and Ajax midfielder, **Edgar Davids**

Chelsea and Milan legend, **Ruud Gullit**

When he was a boy, all Virgil wanted to do was

PLAY FOOTBALL.

He played in the **street**, in the **park**,

at **school**, after **school**

WHEREVER AND WHENEVER HE COULD!

Virgil always had a
ball at his feet.

In football, **forwards** score goals.

They get the **glory** and the **fans**.

Just like every other **football-loving** kid, Virgil wanted to be a **goalscorer**, too!

He wanted to play like the Brazilian superstar **Ronaldinho.**

When he was **seven**, Virgil started playing at his local club, **WDS'19**. He **ALWAYS** wanted the ball, wherever it was on the pitch . . .

THIS KID'S A **DEFENDER**, NOT A STRIKER!

Virgil spent **most of his time** at the local **Cruyff Court**. These special pitches were set up for children all over the Netherlands by the famous Dutch player, **Johan Cruyff**.

The rules of playing in a Cruyff Court match were that the **winner stays on.** The games were very tough, but Virgil loved **showing off his skills.**

Virgil soon became very well known on the **Cruyff Courts** and at **WDS'19**.

CHAPTER 3

WELCOME TO WILLEM II

When Virgil was **TEN**, he had a trial at the local professional team, **NAC Breda**.

It was **VERY** different from WDS'19 and he didn't like it.

Virgil tried out for **Willem II** instead. The club was based in the town of Tilburg, a short train ride from his home.

Virgil's **first few years** at **Willem II** were great, but things started to go wrong when he was about 16.

He wasn't **tall enough** to play in his favourite **centre-back** position.

Virgil was always **cool and calm**,

but sometimes he was **TOO** calm,

and made mistakes.

Virgil wondered what he would do if he **didn't make it as a footballer**. He'd need to **earn money** somehow, so he got a job **washing dishes** at a restaurant in Breda.

Then, when he was **17**, Virgil suddenly grew **A LOT** taller.

HE WAS HUGE!

There was a **problem** with **growing tall** so quickly. It made his bones and muscles ache – **a lot!** Virgil had to work on his fitness and get used to his new size.

It worked! Soon Virgil was

BIGGER, BETTER, FASTER AND STRONGER.

Virgil had grown into an awesome **central defender**. Now, when he played for the **Willem II under-17s**, hardly anyone scored against them.

When Virgil moved to the **Under-19s,** he was made **captain.**

CHAPTER 4

ON TO GRONINGEN

Willem II were never sure that there was a place for Virgil at the club. So just before his **nineteenth birthday**, he signed for **Groningen.**

Groningen was a **long way** from **Breda**, but it was a brilliant team for young players.

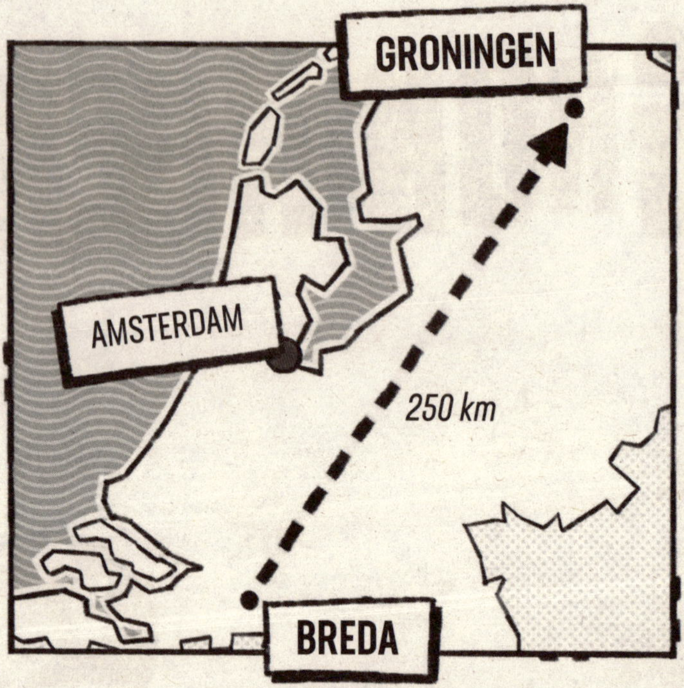

Legendary Dutch **centre-back, Ronald Koeman,** began his career at **Groningen.**
Ronald Koeman
(NOW THE MANAGER OF BARCELONA)

Virgil was living **away from home** for the first time. He missed his **family and friends**.

He had to **cycle** a long way to training, but for Virgil, it was all worth it to **make it** as a footballer.

Virgil was **desperate** to play in the **first team**, but his youth coach **Dick Lukkien** made him wait.

YOU NEED TO TRAIN HARDER.
YOU NEED TO GET STRONGER.
So he did.

Virgil finally made his debut for **Groningen** on **1 May 2011.** He came on as a substitute in an **Eredivisie** game against **ADO Den Haag.**

A few weeks later, Groningen played **Den Haag** again in a **Europa League play-off**. Groningen needed lots of goals, so the manager put **Virgil up front!**

Virgil had a brilliant season, until in **March 2012**, he became **very unwell**. He was rushed to hospital to have his **appendix** removed.

Afterwards, Virgil's doctors, coaches – **and his mum** – all told him that he needed to **eat healthily.**

VAN DIJK'S GRONINGEN RECORD

APPEARANCES	GOALS	ASSISTS
66	7	5

CHAPTER 5

THE BIG MAN

Virgil is tall – VERY tall.
Only 1.7 metres
LIONEL MESSI
RAHEEM STERLING

At **1.93 metres**, he towers over his opponents!

Virgil is a **WORLD CLASS** defender.

He's one of the best at:

Recovering the ball

Tackling

Super-tall Virgil is a **superb header** of the ball – often straight into the goal!

Not all defenders can **pass the ball** well,

but Virgil is an expert at passing.

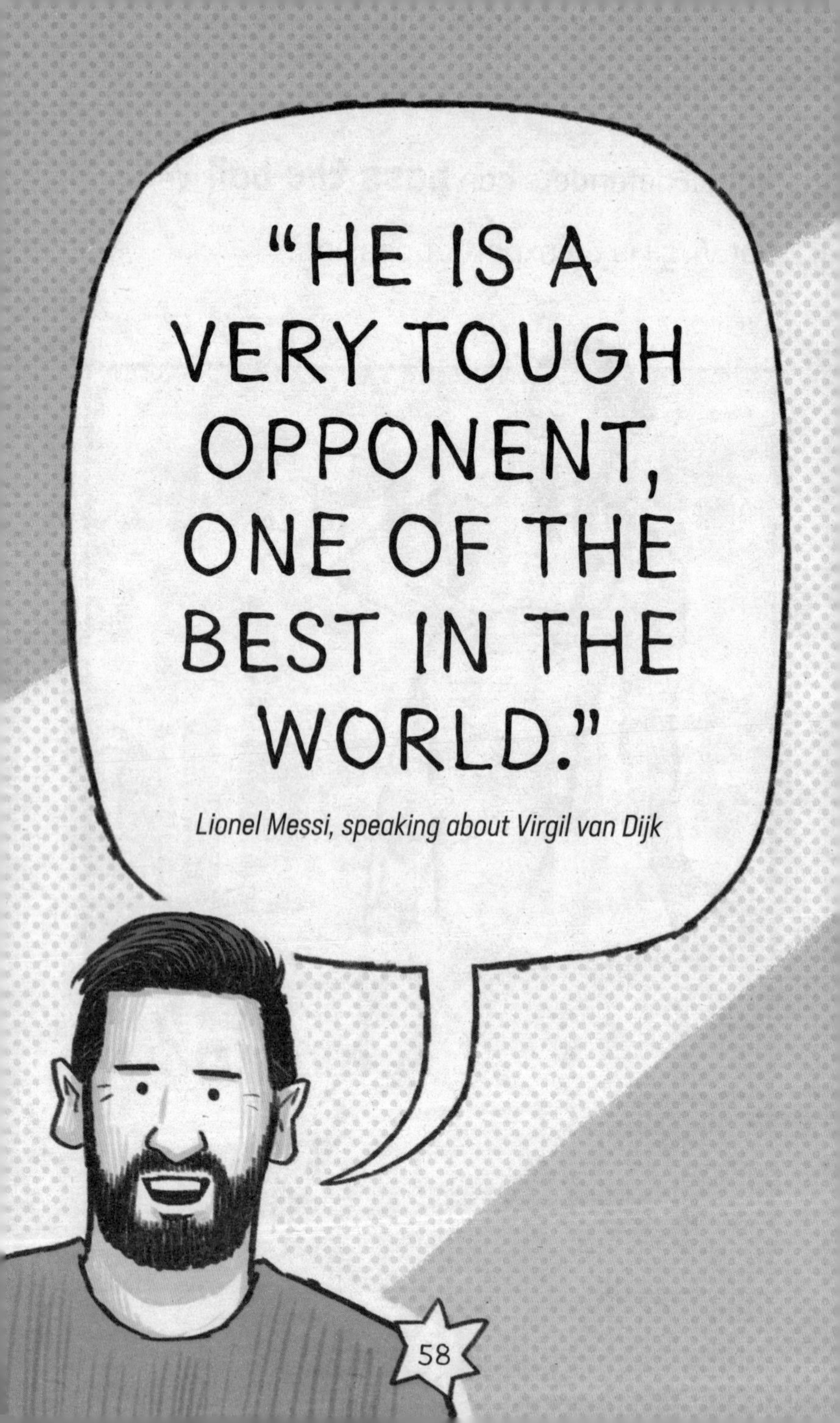
"HE IS A VERY TOUGH OPPONENT, ONE OF THE BEST IN THE WORLD."
Lionel Messi, speaking about Virgil van Dijk

CHAPTER 6

GOING TO GLASGOW

The big Dutch clubs **Ajax** and **PSV Eindhoven** looked at signing Van Dijk, but in **July 2013**, he decided to move move to **another country.**

Virgil signed for the famous Scottish club **Celtic** for an estimated ***£2.6 MILLION.***

VIRGIL
5

CELTIC HIGHLIGHTS

9 NOVEMBER 2013

SCOTTISH PREMIERSHIP

ROSS COUNTY 1-4 CELTIC

Virgil scored his first ***TWO Celtic goals*** *– both of them were headers.*

6 DECEMBER 2013

SCOTTISH PREMIERSHIP

MOTHERWELL 0-5 CELTIC

This game was the ***FIRST*** *in a run of* ***13 CLEAN SHEETS*** *for Virgil and Celtic in the league.* ***Awesome defending!***

15 MARCH 2015

SCOTTISH LEAGUE CUP FINAL

DUNDEE UTD 0-2 CELTIC

*Virgil's first cup final ended in **VICTORY** in front of **50,000 fans** at **Hampden Park.***

WHAT A SHOT!
AYE.
THUMP!

It was at Celtic that Virgil became a free-kick master. He scored an ***ABSOLUTE SCORCHER*** against **Hibernian** in January 2014.

VAN DIJK'S CELTIC RECORD

APPEARANCES	GOALS	ASSISTS
115	15	7

Celtic kept **58 clean sheets** when Virgil was on the pitch.

Virgil won two **Scottish Premierships** and one **Scottish League Cup** at Celtic.

CHAPTER 7

PREMIER CLASS

Virgil **loved Celtic**, but after two seasons, he felt he needed a **new challenge.**

In September 2015, he signed for **Southampton** and became a **Premier League player.**

Dutch legend **Ronald Koeman** was the Southampton manager.

These players were at Southampton, too:

DUŠAN TADIĆ

(Played with Virgil at Groningen)

SADIO MANÉ

(Virgil's Liverpool team-mate!)

DEBUT SEASON HIGHLIGHTS

26 SEPTEMBER 2015

PREMIER LEAGUE

SOUTHAMPTON 3-1 SWANSEA CITY

In his third Premier League game, Virgil scored his ***first Southampton goal*** *after just 11 minutes.*

26 DECEMBER 2015

PREMIER LEAGUE

SOUTHAMPTON 4-0 ARSENAL

*Virgil helped Southampton keep a **clean sheet** as they scored **FOUR** goals against Arsenal. A great present for the fans on Boxing Day!*

23 JANUARY 2016

PREMIER LEAGUE

MANCHESTER UTD 0-1 SOUTHAMPTON

*Virgil helped stop **Wayne Rooney** and **Anthony Martial** scoring at **Old Trafford.** A great win for Southampton.*

Southampton ended the season in **SIXTH** place – their highest finish for **31 years!**

In **November 2016**, Southampton met Italian giants **Inter Milan** in the **Europa League.**

It was a massive night for Virgil.

Southampton were **1–0 down at half-time**, but Virgil urged his players forward.

And then – in the **64th minute**, Virgil scored!

Southampton fought on and eventually won **2–1.**

A FAMOUS VICTORY!

Virgil was a **fan-favourite** at Southampton. They voted him their **player of the year** in his first season and he was made **captain** in **January 2017.**

VIRGIL
17
BUT HOW LONG
WOULD HE STAY?

VAN DIJK'S SOUTHAMPTON RECORD

APPEARANCES	GOALS
80	7
ASSISTS	**CLEAN SHEETS**
0	28

CHAPTER 8

DUTCH DEFENDER

Virgil's **Premier League** performances won him a call-up to the **Netherlands** national side. His debut came in a **EURO 2016** qualifier against **Kazakhstan.**

Sadly, the Netherlands **did not qualify** for that tournament, or the **2018 World Cup!**

But then in 2018 the Netherlands had a new coach. It was Virgil's old Southampton manager, **Ronald Koeman!** He made Virgil his captain.

Virgil's **second game** as captain was a **friendly** against Portugal. Not even **Cristiano Ronaldo** could get past Virgil, and he scored in a **3–0 win.**

In the **2019 Nations League,** Virgil captained an exciting squad that included . . .

The Netherlands beat **Germany, France** and **England** to reach the final, where they lost **1–0** to **Portugal.**

DUTCH GIANTS

Virgil is the latest in a long line of great Dutch defenders.

Jaap Stam 1992-2007

Won the Treble with Manchester United in 1999.

Frank Rijkaard 1980-1995

Ajax legend who won the 1988 European Championship.

Frank de Boer 1988-2006

Captained the Netherlands to the semi-finals at the 1998 World Cup and EURO 2000.

Ronald Koeman 1980-1997

Koeman won every trophy with Barcelona and PSV Eindhoven . . . and managed Virgil!

Virgil's side finished **SECOND** in their **EURO 2020** qualifying group to reach their first major tournament since 2014.

VAN DIJK'S NETHERLANDS RECORD

APPEARANCES	GOALS
35	4
ASSISTS	**CLEAN SHEETS**
0	13

CHAPTER 9

LIVERPOOL

At the age of **26**, Virgil was at the **peak** of his career. And one of the **biggest, most famous clubs in the world** wanted to sign him.

So, in January 2018, Virgil joined

The fee was an estimated ***£75 MILLION*** –

a world record at the time for a defender!*

The Liverpool manager **Jürgen Klopp** was building a team to win **trophies**. He had already signed some **awesome** players such as . . .

Liverpool needed a new centre-back and

Virgil was just the man.

THE BIG DEBUT

5 JANUARY 2018

FA CUP THIRD ROUND

LIVERPOOL 2-1 EVERTON

Virgil's first game for **The Reds** was an **FA Cup** tie against their fierce local rivals, **Everton**. Liverpool had taken the lead but Everton fought back to make it **1-1.**

Virgil played his usual game – defending, but still **pressing forward**. Then in the 84th minute, Liverpool had a **corner** and

BANG!

Virgil was there to head it in.

EUROPEAN DREAMS

Liverpool had reached the knockout stage of the **Champions League** for the first time in seven years. There were some **massive games** to play.

14 FEBRUARY 2018

CHAMPIONS LEAGUE LAST 16 1ST LEG

PORTO 0-5 LIVERPOOL

*A **Sadio Mané hat-trick**, one goal each from **Mo Salah** and **Roberto Firmino** and no goals conceded. Perfect.*

4 APRIL 2018

CHAMPIONS LEAGUE QUARTER-FINAL 1ST LEG

LIVERPOOL 3-0 MANCHESTER CITY

Liverpool destroyed their rivals with ***three first-half goals*** *and kept another clean sheet.*

2 MAY 2018

CHAMPIONS LEAGUE SEMI-FINAL 2nd LEG

ROMA 4-2 LIVERPOOL

The Reds were **5-2** *up from the first leg, but this dramatic game saw them go through* ***7-6 on aggregate.***

26 MAY 2018

CHAMPIONS LEAGUE FINAL

OLYMPIC STADIUM, KIEV

Liverpool faced the mighty **Real Madrid** in the final. Real Madrid have won the trophy more times than any other team.

Liverpool's keeper **Lorius Karius** had a terrible game and **Mo Salah** was injured in a battle with **Sergio Ramos.**

Liverpool lost **3–1.** What a bad night!

But Virgil and his **team-mates** promised one another they would come back **stronger.**

VAN DIJK'S 2017-2018 LIVERPOOL RECORD

APPEARANCES	GOALS	ASSISTS	CLEAN SHEETS
22	1	0	9

CHAPTER 10

LEAGUES AHEAD

PREMIER LEAGUE 2018-19

There were some huge games in Virgil's first **full season** with Liverpool in the **Premier League.** Could The Reds be the **champions?**

16 DECEMBER 2018

LIVERPOOL 3-1 MANCHESTER UNITED

This victory over United put Liverpool at the ***top of the league****, above Man City.* ***A big game*** *and an important win.*

29 DECEMBER 2018

LIVERPOOL 5-1 ARSENAL

*Another big Christmas win at **Anfield.** Virgil and the defence only let **Arsenal** score once. A **Firmino hat-trick** and a goal each from **Salah** and **Mané** saw off the Londoners.*

27 FEBRUARY 2019

LIVERPOOL 5-0 WATFORD

__Virgil, Trent Alexander-Arnold__ and __Andy Robertson__ led the attack from the back to crush Watford. __Two__ of the __FIVE__ goals were headed in by Virgil.

Liverpool and **Manchester City** were fighting for the title all season. But in the end, City won it on the final day - by one point!

POSITION	TEAM	POINTS
1	MANCHESTER CITY	98
2	LIVERPOOL	97
3	CHELSEA	72
4	TOTTENHAM HOTSPUR	71
5	ARSENAL	70
6	MANCHESTER UNITED	66

Liverpool had only lost **one league game** - to Man City.

Liverpool had the **most points** of any team ever to **finish second!**

CHAMPIONS LEAGUE 2018-19

There were some **EPIC** European matches for Virgil and Liverpool during the Champions League in 2018-19. Having ***just*** got out of the group stage despite **LOSING** three games, they saw off **Bayern Munich** and **Porto** to reach the semi-final . . . against **Barcelona.**

They lost the first leg **3-0.**

In the **second leg** they had to score at least **FOUR** goals, and not let **Lionel Messi** and his team-mates score any.

And incredibly, with the Anfield crowd roaring them on, **they did just that!**

KINGS OF EUROPE

In the final, they met their familiar opponents – **TOTTENHAM HOTSPUR**. Thanks to goals from **Mo Salah** and **Divock Origi** Liverpool won **2–0.**

Virgil soon forgot about the disappointment against Madrid a year earlier– he had a **Champions League** medal.

INCREDIBLE!

Champions
LIVERPOOL

VIRGIL WAS A WORLD CLASS PLAYER.

In 2019, he was runner-up in the **Ballon d'Or.**

The only player in the world voted better than Virgil . . . was **Lionel Messi.**

Lionel Messi

VAN DIJK'S 2018-2019 RECORD

APPEARANCES	GOALS
50	6
ASSISTS	**CLEAN SHEETS**
4	26

"THE BEST PLAYER OF ALL? THAT'S LIONEL MESSI. THE BEST PLAYER OF LAST SEASON? THAT'S VIRGIL."

Jürgen Klopp, November 2019

CHAPTER 11

CHAMPION

2019-20 HIGHLIGHTS

THIS WAS A SEASON LIKE NO OTHER.

9 AUGUST 2019

PREMIER LEAGUE

LIVERPOOL 4-1 NORWICH CITY

*The Reds began the season as they meant to go on, **thrashing** newly promoted **Norwich.** Virgil **scored**, too!*

19 JANUARY 2020

PREMIER LEAGUE

LIVERPOOL 2-0 MANCHESTER UTD

*A goal each from **Virgil** and **Mo Salah** and no goals conceded. A **great win** against Liverpool's old rivals.*

11 MARCH 2020

CHAMPIONS LEAGUE

LIVERPOOL 2-3 ATLETICO MADRID

*Not a highlight, but a **big game.** Liverpool were out of the **Champions League**, but it was also the last match they would play for more than **THREE months!***

Liverpool were way ahead at the top of the league. Then in **March 2020**, all football matches stopped because of the **Coronavirus lockdown.**

For **more than a month,** the players couldn't even train together, while their fans waited and hoped. **Would the league start again?**

In **June**, football came back - but the **fans** had to **stay at home.**

On **25 June 2020,** Chelsea beat **Manchester City.** This meant that nobody could catch **Liverpool** - they had won the **Premier League** with a record-breaking **SEVEN games** to go!

Virgil had a **Premier League medal** to add to his **Champions League** one.

VAN DIJK'S 2019-2020 RECORD

APPEARANCES	GOALS
50	5

ASSISTS	CLEAN SHEETS
2	20

CHAPTER 12

VAN THE MAN

It didn't take long for Virgil to become a huge **hero** for the fans in **The Kop**. They made up a **song** for him:

"HE'S A CENTRE-HALF,
HE'S A NUMBER FOUR.

"WATCH HIM DEFEND,
AND WE WATCH HIM SCORE.

"HE'LL PASS THE BALL,
CALM AS YOU LIKE.

"HE'S VIRGIL VAN DIJK,
HE'S VIRGIL VAN DIJK."

Now *Virgil* is on course to becoming a true **Liverpool legend!**
VIRGIL
4

TROPHIES AND AWARDS

VIRGIL HAS WON A **LOT** OF TROPHIES AND AWARDS. THESE ARE SOME OF THEM!

SCOTTISH PREMIERSHIP
2013-14
2014-15

PREMIER LEAGUE
2019-20

CHAMPIONS LEAGUE
2018-19

CLUB WORLD CUP
2019

SUPER CUP
2019

PFA PLAYERS' PLAYER OF THE YEAR 2018-19
PFA PLAYER OF THE MONTH NOVEMBER 2018
CELTIC PLAYERS' PLAYER OF THE YEAR 2013-15
PREMIER LEAGUE PLAYER OF THE SEASON 2018-19
SOUTHAMPTON PLAYER OF THE SEASON 2015-16
UEFA MEN'S PLAYER OF THE YEAR 2018-19

QUIZ TIME!

How much do you know about VIRGIL VAN DIJK? Try this quiz to find out, then test your friends!

1. Where was Virgil born?

---

2. Which Brazilian striker was Virgil's hero when he was a boy?

---

3. What are the special pitches in the Netherlands called where Virgil played?

---

4. Which team did he sign for at the age of ten?

---

5. What job did Virgil do as a teenager?

---

6. Which team did he move away from home to sign for?

---

7. How much did Celtic sign him for in 2013?

---

8. How many times did Virgil win the Scottish Premiership?

---

9. Which Dutch manager signed him at Southampton?

---

10. Which team did Liverpool beat in the 2019 Champions League final?

The answers are on the next page ***but no peeking!***

ANSWERS

1. Breda, The Netherlands
2. Ronaldinho
3. Cruyff Courts
4. Willem II
5. Dishwasher
6. Groningen
7. £2.6 million
8. Twice
9. Ronald Koeman
10. Tottenham Hotspur

VIRGIL VAN DIJK:
WORDS YOU NEED TO KNOW

Premier League
The top football league in England.

Clean Sheet
When a team manages to stop its opponent from scoring any goals.

PFA
Professional Footballers' Association

Eredivisie
The top football league in the Netherlands.

UEFA Champions League
European club competition held every year. The winner is the best team in Europe.

UEFA Europa League
The second-tier European club competition.

ABOUT THE AUTHORS

Simon's first job was at the Science Museum, making paper aeroplanes and blowing bubbles big enough for your dad to stand in. Since then he's written all sorts of books about the stuff he likes, from dinosaurs and rockets, to llamas, loud music and of course, football. Simon has supported Ipswich Town since they won the FA Cup in 1978 (it's true - look it up) and once sat next to Rio Ferdinand on a train. He lives in Kent with his wife and daughter, two tortoises and a cat.

Dan has drawn silly pictures since he could hold a crayon. Then he grew up and started making books about stuff like trucks, space, people's jobs, *Doctor Who* and *Star Wars*. Dan remembers Ipswich Town winning the FA Cup but he didn't watch it because he was too busy making a Viking ship out of brown paper. As a result, he knows more about Vikings than football. Dan lives in Suffolk with his wife, son, daughter and a dog that takes him for very long walks.